I0606187

SCIENTIFIC AMERICAN EDUCATIONAL PUBLISHING

MIND GAMES

10 FUN OPTICAL ILLUSIONS AND PERCEPTION PROJECTS

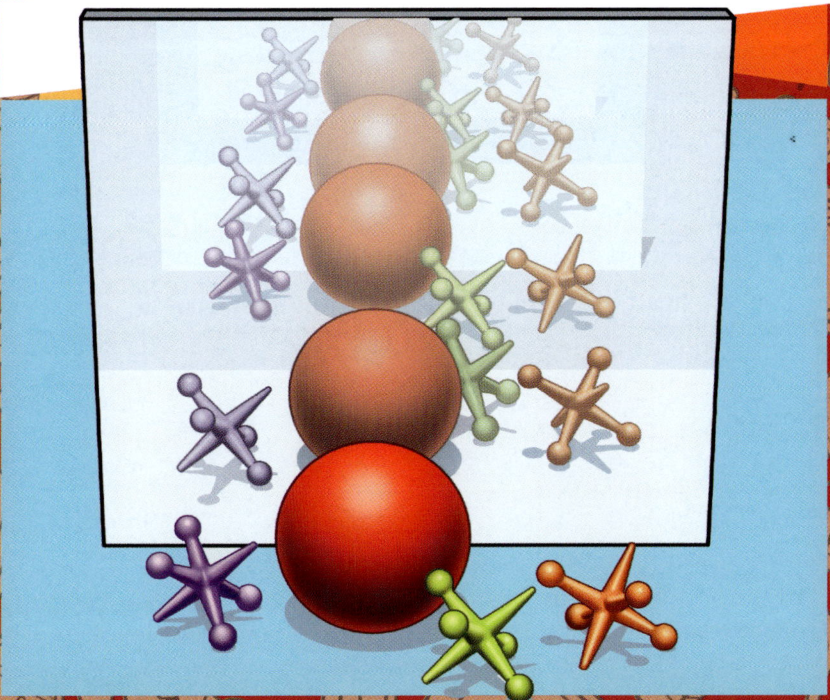

BRING SCIENCE HOME

Published in 2023 by Scientific American Educational Publishing in association with The Rosen Publishing Group
29 East 21st Street, New York, NY 10010

Contains material from Scientific American , a division of Springer Nature America, Inc., reprinted by permission as well as original material from The Rosen Publishing Group .

First Edition

Designer: Rachel Rising

Activity on page 5 by Science Buddies/Svenja Lohner; page 11 Science Buddies/Svenja Lohner; page 17 by Science Buddies/Sabine de Brabandere; page 23 by Science Buddies/Svenja Lohner; page 29 Science Buddies; page 33 Science Buddies; page 39 Science Buddies; page 45 Science Buddies; page 51 Science Buddies; page 56 Science Buddies.

Illustrations by Continuum Content Solutions

Photo Credits: pp.3,-5, 8, 11, 14, 17, 20, 21, 23, 27, 29, 32, 33, 37, 39, 42, 45, 48, 51, 53, 54, 56, 59, 60 cve iv/ Shutterstock.com; pp. 4, 5, 11, 17, 23, 29, 33, 39, 45, 51, 56 Anna Frajtova/Shutterstock.com.

Cataloging-in-Publication Data
Names: Scientific American, inc.
Title: Mind games : 10 fun optical illusions and perception projects / edited by the Editors of Scientific American.
Description: New York : Scientific American Educational Publishing, 2023. | Series: Bring science home | Includes glossary and index.
Identifiers: ISBN 9781684169603 (pbk.) | ISBN 9781684169610 (library bound) | ISBN 9781684169627 (ebook)
Subjects: LCSH: Optical illusions--Experiments--Juvenile literature. | Optical illusions--Juvenile literature.
Classification: LCC QP495.M563 2023 | DDC 152.14'8--dc23

Manufactured in the United States of America

CPSIA Compliance Information: Batch #SACS23. For further information contact Rosen Publishing, New York, New York at 1-800-237-9932.

CONTENTS

INTRODUCTION

People rely on their senses to help them navigate the world. However, these senses aren't foolproof. Certain things can trick the brain into thinking it sees, feels, or tastes something other than what is really there. Use the experiments in this book to find out how this happens.

Projects marked with ⚛ include a section called Science Fair Project ideas. These ideas can help you develop your own original science fair project. Science fair judges tend to reward creative thought and imagination, and it helps if you are really interested in your project. You will also need to follow the scientific method. See page 61 for more information about that.

Find Your Blind Spot!

NOW YOU SEE IT... TRY THIS SIMPLE ACTIVITY TO LOCATE YOUR OWN BLIND SPOTS.

Did you know that you have a blind spot in each of your eyes? This doesn't mean you see a constant black spot in your field of vision. Normally you don't notice these blind spots at all. There are, however, some ways you can make these blind spots come to light, so to speak! This activity will show you how to find them.

PROJECT TIME

15 to 25 minutes

KEY CONCEPTS

Biology
Physiology
Senses
Vision
Perception

BACKGROUND

Our eyes are complex organs that allow us to detect visual objects, colors, motion, and other things happening around us. To be able to see, however, we need light. Usually what we see is light that reflects off of objects and then enters our eyes through the pupil (the pupil is the opening in the middle of the front of the eye). How much light gets into the eye is controlled by the iris, which is the colored part around the pupil that can contract and expand to open and close the pupil. Inside the eye, the light lands on the retina at the back of the eye, which is a light-sensitive layer of tissue. The retina has two types of light-sensing cells: rods and cones. Rods provide black-and-white vision in dim light, whereas cones are responsible for color vision.

When light hits the rod and cone cells, nerve impulses are triggered and sent to the brain through the optic nerve. In humans and most vertebrates, the optic nerve fibers pass through the retina and out of the back of the eyeball. The area where the bundled nerve fibers pass through the retina does not contain any light-sensitive cells. This means we don't see light that hits this exact spot. Although we technically cannot see this light, our brain can usually fill in the information that we are missing based on the other things around the blind spot. This is the reason why we don't usually notice our blind spots. In this activity, however, you will see how under certain circumstances, your blind spot can seem to make things disappear. Are you ready to make your blind spot visible?

MATERIALS

- Cardstock paper
- Scissors
- Ruler or measuring tape
- Pen or pencil

PREPARATION

- Carefully cut a 2-inch-high and 5-inch-long (5 cm by 13 cm) rectangle from the cardstock paper.
- Place the paper rectangle on a surface so that it is lying longways.

- By the left edge of the paper, halfway between the top and bottom, draw a small shape—no wider than 0.5 inch (1 cm)—such as a circle, heart, or plus sign.
- By the right edge, halfway between the top and bottom, draw another shape of approximately the same size.

PROCEDURE

- Take the rectangle in your right hand. Hold it in the middle so you can see both shapes.
- Extend your arm with the rectangle at eye level. Focus your eyes on the left shape. *With your eyes still focused on the left shape, can you still see the shape on the right side of the paper?*
- Slowly move your extended arm closer to your face. While moving the paper closer, keep your eyes focused on the left shape. *While moving the paper, can you still see both shapes clearly?*
- Cover your left eye with your left hand. Extend the right arm with the paper at eye level again. Focus your right eye on the left shape. *Can you see the other shape as well?*
- With your left eye covered and your right eye focusing on the left shape, slowly move the paper closer toward your face. Keep focusing your right eye on the left shape. *What happens to the shape on the right side of the paper while you move the paper closer?*
- Now cover your right eye with your right hand. Extend your left arm with the paper and look at the right shape. *Are you able to still see the left shape while focusing on the right shape with your left eye?*
- Again, slowly move the paper closer to you. Keep your left eye focused on the right shape. *What do you notice this time?*

SCIENCE FAIR IDEA

Draw a horizontal line straight across the paper from one edge to the other, running through your two shapes. Repeat the activity. *How do your results change?*

SCIENCE FAIR IDEA

Can you measure the size of your blind spot? Cover one of your eyes, and position the paper at a distance where one of the shapes disappears from your vision. Move a pen across the paper and mark where it disappears in your blind spot from all sides. The markings allow you to measure the size of your blind spot in your field of vision.

SCIENCE FAIR IDEA

Make a new paper card, but this time draw bigger shapes on each side. *Does the activity still work?*

OBSERVATIONS AND RESULTS

Did you find your blind spot? When looking at the paper rectangle with both eyes, you probably always saw both shapes on each side of the paper—even when you moved your arm closer to your body. When you looked with only your right eye directly at the left shape, however, you should have noticed that at some point the right shape disappeared as you moved the paper closer to your face. At this position, the shape just happened to be in your blind spot. This blind spot is there because the optic nerve fibers pass through the back of your retina inside your eye. Where the nerve passes through, there are no cells receiving light. At this tiny spot, which is approximately the size of a pinhead, you are technically blind. You know that you have such a blind spot in both of your eyes because you should have seen the same thing happen when you looked at the right shape with your left eye. This time the left shape should have disappeared.

If you did the science fair activity with the straight line across the card, you should have noticed that the shape still disappeared, but you still saw a continuous straight line all the way to the edge of the paper. This is a great example of how your brain tries to fill in the blanks of the blind spot. Your brain noticed the straight line in the area surrounding your blind spot—and just continued the line even though it technically didn't detect it there. The brain, however, couldn't notice the shape because it was fully inside the blind spot. As a result, the shape disappeared, but the straight line was still visible.

CLEANUP

Put away your materials. Throw out or recycle any unused scraps.

Reading with Your Fingers

CAN YOU FEEL IT? LEARN HOW YOUR FINGERTIPS CAN DECIPHER THE CODE OF LETTERS AND NUMBERS WITH A HOMEMADE BRAILLE MESSAGE.

PROJECT TIME

30 to 45 minutes

KEY CONCEPTS

Biology
Senses
Perception
Touch

Have you ever been in an elevator and wondered what the many little dots on the buttons are for? You can also find these dots in public buildings on room number signs or on ATMs (cash machines). These arrangements of dots are a special writing system for the visually impaired called braille. By feeling the dots with their fingers, people can read what is written on a sign or elevator button. Do you want to find out how to read with your fingers? This activity will show you how!

BACKGROUND

For a long time, being able to see was a prerequisite for reading. No other reading medium was available for people who were blind or had impaired vision. This changed only in the early 1800s when Samuel Gridley Howe, the founder of the New England School for the Blind, created Boston Line Type, the first writing system for the blind. The system was based on a tactile reading code, which means reading by touch, and consisted of an embossed, simplified Roman alphabet.

This type of reading is possible because our fingertips contain a huge network of nerve endings and touch receptors that allow us to detect tiny bumps on a piece of paper. Once these touch receptors are activated by feeling a bump, a signal is sent from the nerves in our fingertips all the way into our brain, which is then able to decode the information we gained by touching the paper.

The braille system was developed by Louis Braille in the 1820s and consists of raised dots arranged in a six-dot cell. A different pattern is assigned to each letter of the alphabet. Braille got this idea from a military code called night writing. Night writing allowed soldiers to communicate during the night without making any sounds or using light. Although several other tactile writing systems have been developed over time, braille was widely adopted and is still in use today. Do you want to test your sense of touch and find out how to read these dots? Grab a piece of paper and get started!

MATERIALS

- Graph paper
- Parchment paper
- Pencil or other pointed object, such as a knitting needle
- Cardboard
- Computer or mobile device with access to the internet
- Tape
- Helper

PREPARATION

- **Look up the braille alphabet on the internet to see which dot pattern stands for each letter.**
- **Place the graph paper on top of the cardboard.**

PROCEDURE

- Choose one square of the graph paper, and gently press down on the paper with the tip of the pencil or knitting needle—being careful not to puncture the paper.

- Flip the graph paper over. *Can you see the raised bump in the paper?* Run your index fingertip over the punched spot. *How does it feel? What letter does one dot stand for?*

- Repeat this step, but this time choose two squares next to each other and punch one dot lightly onto the paper with the tip of the pencil in each square. *When you flip your paper over, can you feel both bumps next to each other with your fingertips? Which letter does your chosen dot pattern stand for?*

- Next, place the parchment paper onto the graph paper and tape them together. Think of an entire word to write. With the help of the braille alphabet you found online, draw the corresponding dot patterns for your word onto your parchment paper. The graph paper underneath will help you keep the dots in line.

- Place the graph paper on top of the cardboard, flip over the parchment paper, and lay it on top of the graph paper.

- Press on each dot of your dot pattern written on the parchment paper to create bumps in the graph paper underneath. Once you are done, flip your graph paper around and try to read the word with your fingers. *Are you able to make out the individual letters? Can you read the whole word? Does it make a difference if you read with your eyes closed or open?*

- Ask your helper to create a single letter dot pattern for you the same way you did in the first step. They should keep the letter secret from you. Once your helper has completed the dot pattern, check the braille alphabet once more, and then close your eyes. Try to identify the letter with your fingertips without looking. *Can you identify the correct letter?*

- Repeat this challenge as many times as you like—or make it more difficult and ask your helper to write a whole word in braille for you. *Can you read the word with closed eyes?*

SCIENCE FAIR IDEA

Does it make a difference which fingertip you use for reading? Try using your middle finger or pinky instead of your index finger and see which finger is best at identifying the writing.

SCIENCE FAIR IDEA

You can also read braille with two hands. Braille readers use the index fingers of both the left and right hands simultaneously to reduce their reading time. *How does reading with one hand compare to reading with two hands?*

SCIENCE FAIR IDEA

Try to change the spacing between your dots. *Can you read your letters better if the dots are closer to one another or farther apart?*

OBSERVATIONS AND RESULTS

Were you able to read with your fingers? It can be quite challenging if you are not used to it. However, you should have been able to feel the bumps on the graph paper that you made with your pencil. If you run your index finger across the paper, the touch receptors in your fingertips recognize the difference between the flat paper and the bump. This triggers your receptors, and they send a signal from the nerves in your fingertips to your brain. This way you know how many bumps you felt on the paper and in which position in the six-dot cell they were.

Usually the index fingers are used to read braille, although the other fingers should also have been able to identify the bumps. It makes a difference how close or far apart you space the individual dots. If they are too far away, one fingertip alone is not able to detect them anymore. If they are too close together, your finger might not be able to identify them as two separate dots. Now that you know how braille works, try reading it with your fingers the next time you see it!

CLEANUP

Put your materials back where you found them.

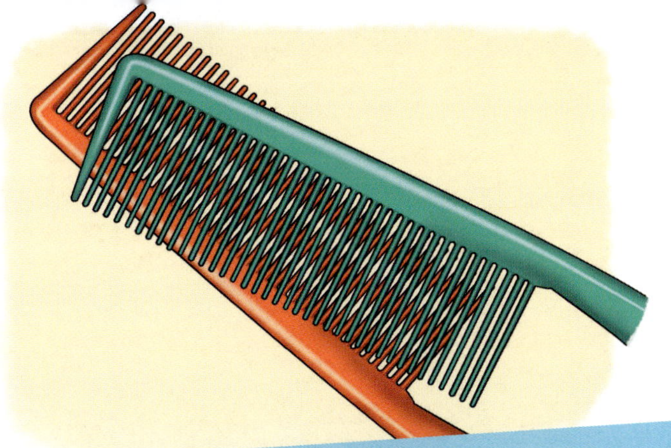

Interfering Patterns

CAN YOU TRICK YOUR EYES WITH THESE GROOVY MATHEMATICAL PATTERNS? GRAB A FEW HOUSEHOLD ITEMS AND FIND OUT!

Have you ever wondered why our eyes are drawn to patterns? We see patterns in art and music, and also in our daily lives. Patterns can provide a sense of order and can make a hectic-looking world a little more manageable. They are the basis of many assumptions and predictions. We assume we will have lunch at noon if that is what we always do. We predict thunderclouds will bring rain. And you might expect to get in trouble when you disobey the rules. We are so used to looking for patterns that we might even see one where there is none. In this activity, we look for one of those illusions: one that printers avoid but scientists have put to good use.

PROJECT TIME

25 to 30 minutes

KEY CONCEPTS

Mathematics
Patterns
Interference
Optical illusion

BACKGROUND

Sometimes the whole is more than the sum of its parts. This is definitely true with interference patterns, which are the result of waves intersecting in a constructive or destructive way. In acoustics, interference of two waves with slightly different frequencies creates a beat, or a periodic variation in volume. In optics, the double-slit experiment showed that the interference of two slightly displaced light waves of the same frequency gives rise to a series of alternating dark and bright bands. A lesser-known interference pattern—the moiré interference pattern—occurs when a regular pattern with transparent gaps overlaps another similar pattern. The two patterns must *almost* exactly overlap or be *almost* identical. A small displacement, rotation, or difference in period, etc., is essential for the interference pattern to occur.

Moiré patterns are the enemy of many: In printing, arrangements of dots can create unwelcome moiré patterns; in television and digital photography, a pattern on an object can interfere with the pattern of the light sensors or camera sensors, adding unwanted moiré patterns to the picture. Scientists, on the other hand, have managed to use moiré patterns to their advantage in tools to make microscopic measurements. Moiré patterns are attractive there because the periodicity of the created pattern magnifies the tiny differences of the interfering patterns.

MATERIALS

- Pocket combs (At least two should be identical or have pins that are almost identical in thickness and spacing.)
- Two screens, such as window screens, at least one of which you can manipulate freely
- Nylon stockings
- Surface or background that is a contrasting color to your materials to help spot the patterns

PREPARATION

- Gather your materials together in your work space.

PROCEDURE

- Start with the pair of combs. Place them separately on a contrasting background. *How would you describe the pattern of pins? Is it regular or irregular? Are the pins spaced far apart or close to one another?*

- *If you place two identical combs exactly on top of each other so they perfectly overlap, how do you expect the pattern of pins you observed to change? Would it be any different if you make the two combs almost perfectly line up?*

- Test your prediction. If you do not have two identical combs, use two that are very similar in their pin patterns. *Do you see what you predicted?*

- If the combs are slightly misaligned or if their pattern of pins is slightly different, you should see a third pattern occur: one that has a distance between repeating parts that is several times the distance between the individual pins of the combs. If you cannot see it, try a different combination of combs or switch the top comb with the bottom one. Having a contrasting background can help as well.

- Shift the top comb slowly side to side. *What do you observe now?*

- Rotate the combs over a small angle with respect to each other. *Does the pattern change? What happens if you increase the angle of rotation?* (Hint: Pay attention to the distance between the repeated parts of the appearing pattern.)

- Test different combinations of combs to find out what is necessary to make these patterns appear.

- You just explored overlapping patterns of parallel lines. *Do you think the same thing would happen if you overlapped other patterns, such as patterns of squares?*

- Look at a window screen. *Do you see the pattern of squares?* Notice that the size of a square determines the distance between the repeating parts of this pattern.
- Observe a second window screen. *Does it have squares of a similar size?*
- Think for a moment. *How would you place the two screens together to create a third pattern?* Think about how this is similar and how it is different from your comb experiment.
- If you can, try it out. *Does a new pattern appear?*
- *How do the patterns change when you change the angle of rotation between the screens?*
- Imagine shrinking the squares in the window screen until they are tiny. *Would it almost look like looking through a single layer of nylon stocking? Do you think you can create patterns by overlapping layers of nylon stockings? Why or why not?*
- Perform the test. Look through two layers of nylon against an even, contrasting background. *Do you see patterns occur? How are they similar and how are they different from the patterns you saw earlier?*

SCIENCE FAIR IDEA

What you observed in this activity are moiré patterns. *Can you find other moiré patterns around the house, such as folded thin curtains or, when outside, driving or walking around town?* Pay attention to chain-link fences. The fence and its shadow can even combine to create a moiré pattern. Watch how the patterns change as you move.

SCIENCE FAIR IDEA

Use a computer printer and print identical patterns of lines or concentric circles on two transparencies. *Can you create artistic moiré patterns by shifting or rotating these transparencies with respect to each other?*

SCIENCE FAIR IDEA

Use an online moiré pattern generator to create some nice patterns. Try to predict how the pattern will change when you change one of the parameters.

OBSERVATIONS AND RESULTS

Did you see patterns appear when two identical (or almost identical) repetitive patterns overlapped? Did the distance between repetitive parts decrease as you increased the angle of rotation?

The appearing patterns are called moiré patterns. They amplify small differences between two identical or almost identical repetitive patterns. If you had identical combs and could exactly line them up, no moiré pattern should have been visible. It is the small differences in pattern or the small misalignment that gives rise to clearly visible longer-range moiré patterns. Did you notice that an increase in misalignment—a larger shift, a larger angle of rotation, or a bigger difference in initial patterns—made the distance between repetitive parts in the moiré pattern decrease? Once the differences in the two initial patterns or the misalignments are too big, you can no longer detect the moiré pattern.

Moiré patterns are not really there; they are an optical illusion created in the image in your eye.

CLEANUP

Put your materials back where you found them.

Sensing with Your Feet!

WHAT OBJECTS CAN YOU IDENTIFY WITH YOUR EYES CLOSED? WHAT IF YOU CAN ONLY USE YOUR FEET TO FEEL THEM OUT? TRY THIS ACTIVITY FOR SOME SENSATIONAL RESULTS!

How many objects do you think you touch with your hands every day? A lot! Every time you touch something, your hands are able to feel how smooth, cold, warm, or rough the object is. In fact, your hands and fingers are so good at sensing details of shapes and surface textures that you are often able to identify an object just by touch and without seeing it. Here is the challenge, though: Do you think your feet are sensitive enough to do the same? Are they able to identify objects just by touching them? Try this activity to find out!

PROJECT TIME

30 to 45 minutes

KEY CONCEPTS

Biology
Senses
Perception
Receptors

BACKGROUND

When we touch something, we get a lot of information about the object. This is possible because our skin contains an extensive network of nerve endings and touch receptors, which make it sensitive to many different kinds of stimuli. A stimulus can be anything that triggers the receptors in your skin to a response, such as pressure, temperature, vibrations, or pain. Once the receptors are activated by the stimulus, a series of nerve impulses is triggered and transmitted to our brains, which then use this information to identify the object. Just passive contact of an object is not enough to identify it, however. To make out its shape and details, we have to actively explore its surfaces and the object as a whole by moving it in our hands. This is called haptic perception.

To be able to identify an object by just using haptic perception, we use different receptor types that are each responsible for sensing different stimuli. The mechanoreceptors, for example, perceive sensations such as vibrations, pressure, or texture, whereas the thermoreceptors respond to the temperature of an object. Special pain receptors are responsible for picking up anything that has the potential to damage the skin, and proprioceptors can sense the position of different parts of the body in relation to one another and the surrounding environment. These sensors in combination allow us to pick up an object's shape and temperature as well as its surface texture just by touching it. The gathered information then makes it possible for our brains to identify it.

Why are we able to identify an object just with our hands? Is it because we had a lifetime of experience seeing objects in front of us as we touched them? Did this combination of visual and haptic perception wire our brains in a way that it is able to combine these two sensory inputs? Are we evolutionary conditioned to "see" with our hands? There is an easy experiment to investigate these questions. What if we use another body part to identify a familiar object that has not been trained to do this kind of task: your feet! Do you think your feet can "see"?

MATERIALS

- Chair
- Helper
- Blindfold (such as a scarf)
- About 20 familiar objects to identify, such as toys, foods, household items, clothes, etc.
- (Make sure none of these objects have sharp ends or can break easily. They should be at least the size of your fist or as long as your fingers. Have your helper gather these, and make sure that you do not see them.)

PREPARATION

- Sit on a chair. Your feet should still be able to comfortably reach the ground.
- Let your helper blindfold you.
- Have your helper bring over the 20 familiar objects from your environment.
- You will only have 10 seconds to identify each object, so once you are handed an object, your helper has to slowly count to 10 and then take it away again.

PROCEDURE

- While still blindfolded and sitting on the chair, ask you helper to place one of the objects in your hands. Move the object in both of your hands and explore its shape and texture. *How big is the object? Does it feel warm or cold? Is its surface rough or smooth?*
- As soon as you think you have identified the object, tell your helper your guess and pass it back. *Were you able to identify it within the given 10 seconds? Did you feel it was easy or hard to identify?*
- Once your helper gets the object back, without telling you, they will place the object in a "wrong" pile if you could not identify it and in a "right" pile if you could. This way, you can keep track of your responses.
- After finishing with the first object, repeat the steps with another nine objects, so you have explored a total of 10 objects with both of your hands. *Was there any object that you could not guess in time? How easy or difficult did you find the task? Were there any stimuli that helped you more or less in identifying the object?*

- For the next 10 objects (they should not be the same as the previous ones), you will use your feet to identify them. Remove your shoes and socks so your feet are bare.
- While still blindfolded and sitting, let your helper place one object close to your feet. Then explore the project with your feet and toes and again try to make a guess of the object's identity within the first 10 seconds. *Do you find it easy to explore the object with your feet? Is it easier or harder than using your hands?*
- After 10 seconds, make a guess and let your helper take the object away. Your helper should make two separate piles for the feet experiment depending on if you guessed the object right or wrong.
- Follow the same procedure (just using your feet) to identify the remaining nine objects. *Can you sense details of the object such as surface texture, shape, or temperature with your feet? Were you able to identify all the objects within 10 seconds? Did you have difficulties identifying all of them?*
- Once you have completed identifying all 20 objects (10 with your hands and 10 with your feet), remove your blindfold and look at all the objects. First, let your helper explain to you which objects you guessed right and wrong with your hands. *Did you guess all the objects right? Which ones were difficult or did you get wrong? Can you think of a reason why?*
- Next, let your helper show you which objects you guessed right and wrong with your feet. *How many objects did you guess right, wrong, or were unable to guess in time? Were you able to identify more objects with your hands or your feet within 10-second limit? Can you explain your results?*

SCIENCE FAIR IDEA

In addition to using both of your hands and feet, run the same experiment again (using different objects). This time, only use one hand or one foot to explore the objects. *Is it easier or more difficult compared with using both hands and feet? Does it make a difference if you use your left or right foot or hand?*

SCIENCE FAIR IDEA

Instead of allowing only 10 seconds for each object, take your time until you can make a confident guess of the object's identity. Let your helper time how long you need to identify each object using your hands and feet, respectively. *Do you see any trends in your results? Does it take longer using your hands or feet? Does it depend on the type of object?*

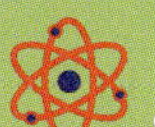

SCIENCE FAIR IDEA

Explore how the object size affects your results. Try the same test with different-size objects. *Which are easier to identify—big objects or small?*

OBSERVATIONS AND RESULTS

Did you get all objects right when exploring them with your hands? You were probably able to identify most of the objects when using both of your hands to touch and feel the object. The receptors in your hands are trained and used to recognizing various stimuli that come from the object, such as its surface texture, shape, and temperature. In combination with the knowledge of how certain objects look and feel, your brain can make a positive identification of the object even though it does not really see it. Ten seconds was probably also long enough to make a good guess for each object—and in case you did not get the object right, it was most likely due to the fact that it was an unfamiliar object that you have not seen or touched that often before.

With your feet, everything gets more complicated. One reason is that your feet have very different anatomy from your hands. Your toes are much shorter than your fingers and much less flexible, which makes it harder to grasp and enclose the object. The other reason is your feet are not used to using their touch receptors to feel and explore objects like your hands are. As a result, you should have noticed that you had more wrong guesses (or could not make a guess in time) when using your feet to identify the object—although you might have been surprised by how many objects you guessed right!

If you measured your response time for each object, you should have found a slower recognition by feet than by hands. Recognition with your feet should have also improved with larger object sizes because small objects are difficult to grasp with your toes. Now that you know that not only your hands but also your feet are capable of identifying objects just by haptics, do you think you can "train" your feet to get as good as your hands?

CLEANUP

Put away the objects you used.

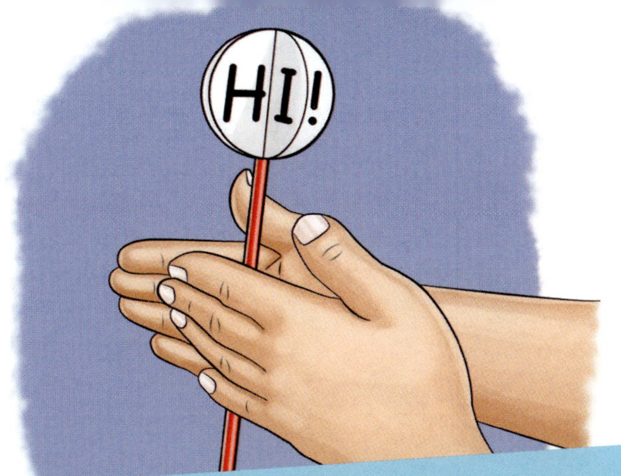

The First Cartoon:
Make Your Own Thaumatrope!

NOW YOU SEE IT—NOW YOU SEE MORE! BUILD THIS CLEVER TOY AND SEE HOW SOME OF THE EARLIEST CARTOONS WERE CREATED. WHAT WILL YOU ANIMATE?

It's probably difficult to imagine a time with no television, no movies, and no cartoons. However, believe it or not, those times weren't so long ago! What did those kids do when they couldn't watch movies? One of the most popular toys during that time was a great-grandfather of the modern cartoon. This toy was called a "thaumatrope," and in this activity, you're going to make (and test) your own thaumatrope to learn about how vision works!

PROJECT TIME

20 to 30 minutes

KEY CONCEPTS

Vision
Perception
Measurement

BACKGROUND

Thaumatropes employ the same science used by the artists that draw your favorite cartoons. While watching a movie, we see characters jumping, running, and dancing instead of seeing hundreds of still images. Our brain takes the images flashing on the screen and connects them to form a continuous stream of motion. This is known as the illusion of apparent motion.

Thaumatropes use the same illusion to join two separate images into one image. They were one of the most popular toys available in the U.S. during the 1920s. Many of the original thaumatropes were made by gluing two pieces of paper together and spinning them on a string. In this activity, you'll use a rod, making it slightly easier to spin. However, feel free to test other designs—see which one works best for you!

MATERIALS

- Chopstick or thin dowel rod (about 1 foot, or 30 cm)
- White paper (Construction paper or stiffer paper type works best.)
- Permanent marker
- Clear tape
- A ruler
- A pencil

PREPARATION

- Cut out two circles from your paper, approximately 2 inches (5 cm) in diameter. For reference, we'll call them "Circle 1" and "Circle 2."
- Find the center of Circle 1 using your ruler. Use your pencil to lightly draw a line across the center.
- Line your ruler up along the line you just drew, then measure 0.25 inch (0.5 cm) from both edges of the circle. Mark the two points with your pencil.
- On the left side of Circle 1, start at the 0.25-inch (0.5 cm) mark and write the letter "H" using your permanent marker. Make the letter large, approximately 1.5 inches (4 cm) tall.

- Starting at the other 0.25-inch point, draw a large "!" with your permanent marker.
- Now begin with Circle 2. Draw a line across the middle of Circle 2.
- Line up your ruler along the line on Circle 2. Measure 1 inch (2.5 cm) from the right side and mark that point with your pencil.
- Use your permanent marker to draw a large letter "I" at the 1-inch (2.5 cm) point on Circle 2.
- Sandwich your dowel rod between the two circles (with the writing facing out). Tape the paper to the rod, and then tape the paper together, creating a paper-and-dowel rod lollipop!
- Hold the rod between both hands with Circle 1 facing you.
- Practice slowly turning the rod by rubbing your hands together so that you see Circle 2, then Circle 1.
- Once you have mastered rotating the circles, you're ready to start!

PROCEDURE

- Hold the rod between both hands with Circle 1 facing you.
- Hum (or sing!) the alphabet song. Rub your hands together to the beat of the song while looking at the circles. *Does anything change about how the letters look? What do you see as you look at the circles?*
- Gradually increase the speed that you rotate the circles. Keep looking at them! *What do you notice as the circles flip faster? Does anything change about how the letters look?*
- Rotate the rod as fast as you can while still looking at the circles. *What do you notice about the letters on the circle?*

- Continue spinning the rod, but try blinking every second. *Does blinking your eyes change the way the letters look? If so, what are the changes?*

Try drawing other things on the circles. For example, draw a fish on Circle 1 and a fishbowl on Circle 2. See what happens!

SCIENCE FAIR IDEA

Try testing the arrangement of letters (or pictures) on the two circles. *What happens when you draw a letter on Circle 1 and a different letter in the same place on Circle 2?*

OBSERVATIONS AND RESULTS

When you rotated the rod at top speed, the letters on the Circle 1 and Circle 2 should have merged together so that you saw the word "HI!". Even though the letters are on two different sides of your "lollipop," when you spin them quickly, your brain doesn't process the two sides as separate images. Instead, it merges them together to create one word!

One reason our brains do this is to help us understand movement in the environment. When you watch a person walk across a room, you don't see every tiny movement that person makes as they walk. Instead, you see a continuous, smooth motion. If you've ever been in a room with a strobe light, you know how important it is that our brains can do this for us. A person dancing under a strobe light can look like a robot because their movements seem disconnected and separate. Our brains can't connect the movements because the light is flashed only at relatively long intervals. You should have observed a similar effect when you watched the spinning circles while blinking. Even though you were spinning the circles at the same speed, your brain couldn't connect the images as it did when your eyes were open.

CLEANUP

Throw away or recycle any unused scraps.

See Change: 2 Eyes, 1 Picture

CAN YOU SEE IT NOW? HOW OUR BRAIN TRANSFORMS TWO PICTURES INTO ONE.

Is catching, juggling, or heading a ball challenging for you? If you've ever tried threading a needle, did it end in frustration? Have you ever thought of blaming your eyes? Two eyes that work together help you estimate how far a ball is or where the thread is with respect to the needle. This "working together" of the eyes actually happens in the brain. The brain receives two images (one for each eye), processes them together with the other information received, and returns one image, resulting in what we "see." Are you curious about how depth perception enters the picture? "See" for yourself with this activity!

PROJECT TIME

10 to 20 minutes

KEY CONCEPTS

Human Body
Binocular vision
Stereopsis
Depth perception
3-D

BACKGROUND

Humans have two eyes, but we only see one image. We use our eyes in synergy (together) to gather information about our surroundings. Binocular (or two-eyed) vision has several advantages, one of which is the ability to see the world in three dimensions. We can see depth and distance because our eyes are located at two different points—about 3 inches (7.5 cm) apart—on our heads. Each eye looks at an item from a slightly different angle and registers a slightly different image on its retina (the back of the eye). The two images are sent to the brain, where the information is processed. In a fraction of a second, our brain brings one three-dimensional (3-D) image to our awareness. The 3-D aspect of the image allows us to perceive width, length, depth, and distance between objects. Scientists refer to this as binocular stereopsis.

Artists use binocular stereopsis to create 3-D films and images. They show each eye a slightly different image. The two images show the objects as seen from slightly different angles, as they would be when seen in real life. For some people, it is easy to fuse two slightly different images presented at each eye; others find it harder. Their depth perception might rely more on other clues. They might find less pleasure in 3-D pictures, movies, or games, and certain tasks—such as threading a needle or playing ball—might be more difficult.

MATERIALS

- Three different-colored markers or highlighters that can easily stand vertically
- Ruler
- Table
- Camera
- Flat work space, such as a tabletop

PREPARATION

- Place the first marker vertically (standing up, as in the picture on page 33) about 1 foot (30 cm) from the edge of the table.
- Place the next marker 1 foot (30 cm) behind it—about 2 feet (60 cm) from the edge—and place the last one 1 foot (30 cm) from the second marker—about 3 feet (91 cm)—from the edge.

If your table is not long enough, you can place your three markers at 6, 12, and 18 inches (15, 30, and 45 cm) from the edge of the table.

PROCEDURE

- Position yourself at the edge of the table and bend your knees so your eye level is at the level of the markers.
- Close or cover your right eye and look only with the left eye. Shift your head so all three markers are right behind the other. *Is it possible to hide the second and third markers behind the first one?*
- Keep the position of your head the same, but now close or cover the left eye and look only with the right eye. *What do you see? In your image, are the second and third markers still hidden behind the first one? Why do you think this happens?*
- Keeping your left eye covered, reposition yourself so the second and third markers are hidden by the first one. Switch the eye with which you are looking again. *Did it happen again?* This time, observe some details. *In your image, is the second marker to the right or the left of your first marker? What about the last marker? How far apart are the markers in your image? Do you see space between the first and the second markers? Do you see as much space between the second and third markers (those that are farther away from you)? Are some markers still partially overlapping?*
- Open or uncover your right eye and look with both eyes. *What do you see? Are any markers hidden by closer markers?* Try to reposition your face so that in your image, the closer marker hides the more distant markers. *Is it easy? Is it even possible?*
- Use a camera to study this in more detail. Position the camera so the first marker hides the second and third markers. The tops of the markers can stick out. Take a picture.

- Shift your camera about 3 inches (7.5 cm) horizontally to the side, and take a second picture. Remember whether you shifted to the right or to the left. If you shift right, the first picture represents what the left eye sees. If you shift left, the first picture represents what your right eye sees.

- Look at the pictures. These images reflect what your right and left eye register. *Are both pictures identical? In what way do they differ?*

- The brain uses the different location of objects in the images received by the right and the left eyes to create depth perception. *Can you find some rules the brain uses? Which marker do you think shifts most with respect to a distant point or with respect to the last marker—the closer one or the one that is farther away?*

- In the first picture, the three markers are lined up. In the second, they are not. Measure how much the second marker is shifted with respect to the last marker. Now measure how much the first marker, which was positioned closer to the camera, is shifted with respect to the last marker. *Does shift increase or decrease when objects are placed farther away from the observer?*

- Look at your second picture. *Is your second marker shifted to the right or the left with respect to the last marker? What about the first marker? Is this direction identical to the direction in which you shifted your camera?*

- *Can you imagine how the picture would look if you shifted the camera by about 3 inches (7.5 cm) to the other side?* You can repeat the part of the procedure where you take the pictures, but now shift your camera to the other side to find out.

SCIENCE FAIR IDEA

Study other parameters that might influence the shift. *Do the markers shift more or less with respect to one another if you (as observer) position yourself farther away from the set of markers? What happens if you gaze at a point far in the background?* (That is, compare the shift with respect to a point in the background.) Pictures can help you perform a more detailed analysis. A row of equally spaced trees, light poles, or other objects along a straight street can also help you perform a more elaborate investigation.

SCIENCE FAIR IDEA

Imagine what would happen if our eyes were separated by a longer horizontal distance. *Do you think the horizontal shift would be larger or smaller? What do you think would happen if our eyes were shifted vertically instead of horizontally?* Take pictures where you position the camera at slightly different locations in space to find out. *Can you find some advantages and disadvantages to having eyes that are separated as they currently are in humans?*

SCIENCE FAIR IDEA

Adequate depth perception facilitates tasks such as playing ball, threading a needle, and driving. To experience how difficult playing ball and threading a needle are with monocular (or one-eyed) vision, cover one eye and perform the task. Be careful, though; this is difficult! Start by throwing a ball softly. Do not perform any dangerous tasks with one eye covered.

OBSERVATIONS AND RESULTS

Did you see how your right eye registers the world differently from your left eye? Did you see how using both eyes created yet a different picture?

When you lined up the markers so your left eye could only see the first one, they were no longer lined up when you looked with the right eye only. Something similar happened when you lined up the markers for your right eye and you switched to a left-eye-only view. This time, the markers were shifted to the right in your image. This happened because each eye looked at the row of markers from a slightly different angle.

With both eyes open, it was probably very hard or impossible to position yourself so you could only see the first marker. Most people have a hard time fusing the images created by each eye in this particular setup. You might have experienced that you switched between images or had double vision.

The pictures you took with the camera allowed you to compare how much a closer marker shifted with respect to a more distant one. If you performed more tests, you might have discovered that the shift depends on the distance between the objects, the distance between you and the objects, and the point you are gazing at (also called the point of focus).

CLEANUP

Put away your materials.

Can You Spot the Dot?

THE AMAZING DISAPPEARING DOT! IT'S NOT MAGIC—IT'S SCIENCE! LEARN HOW YOU CAN FOOL YOUR OWN EYES WITH THIS SURPRISING SCIENCE ACTIVITY.

Have you ever wanted to make something disappear? You might just be able to. Your eyes collect information with quick movements around your environment and pass this information on to your brain. In this activity, we will take advantage of the way your eyes and brain talk to each other to make colored dots seem to appear and disappear. (Sorry, this disappearing act probably won't work on your homework!)

PROJECT TIME

20 to 25 minutes

KEY CONCEPTS

Perception
Color and light
Vision
Eyes

BACKGROUND

You don't realize it, but your eyes are continuously making small, jittery movements. This happens so quickly that we usually can't see or feel it. It's similar to if you use a computer to zoom in on a photo and then scroll over the zoomed image. As you move, you gain more information about the image as a whole.

In our eyes, these movements are called saccades, and they allow your eyes to continuously gather and update information to send to your brain. Among other things, saccades help us see edges, such as the end of a table or the edges of a dot on a piece of paper. Our eyes best detect edges when there is a high degree of contrast in your environment. In general, it's much easier to see the edge of a doorway than the edge of a cloud. The doorway has very precise edges with high contrast, whereas a cloud can have irregular, blurry edges and less contrast.

In this activity, we will see how blurry edges can cause problems for your eyes—and make things seem to disappear!

MATERIALS

- One sheet each of red, blue, green, and orange construction paper
- Scissors
- One sheet of wax paper (approximately 8 by 11 inches, or 20 by 28 cm)
- Ruler
- A partner (to help you measure and record during the activity)

PREPARATION

- Carefully cut each piece of construction paper in half.
- Set one half sheet of each color aside. (We'll refer to these as the "large sheets" in the procedure.)
- Cut a 1-inch (2.5 cm) diameter circle from each of the other half sheets.

PROCEDURE

- Take the large red sheet of construction paper and place it on a flat surface. (A table or countertop works best.)
- Place the orange dot in the center of the red construction paper sheet.
- Place the wax paper down so that it covers the dot and sheet. *Can you still see the orange dot?*
- Slowly lift the wax paper away from the table and toward your face. Keep the wax paper parallel to the table so that it continues to cover the dot and red sheet. Look through the wax paper to the colored paper below. *What do you notice happening to the orange dot as you lift the wax paper?*
- Raise the wax paper until the orange dot becomes fuzzy and faint but is still visible.
- Have your partner use the ruler to measure the distance between the tabletop and the wax paper, then write it down.
- Without moving the wax paper, stare at a point next to the fuzzy orange dot without moving your eyes or your head. Do this for at least 10 seconds. *What do you notice about the orange dot? Does it get easier or more difficult to see?*
- Without moving the wax paper, move your eyes or your head slightly. *What do you notice about the orange dot when you move your eyes or head? Does it get easier or more difficult to see?*
- Repeat the activity with the green dot on the red paper, then the blue dot on the red paper. Measure the height of the wax paper above the dot each time. *Is the height the same for each color, or can you move the wax paper higher and still see the dot for some colors?*

SCIENCE FAIR IDEA

When you get to the point in the activity when you're focusing on a point next to the dot, try moving the wax paper up and down without moving your eyes. *Does the appearance of the dot change as you move the paper? Does it get easier to see?*

SCIENCE FAIR IDEA

When you get to the point in the activity when you're focusing on a point next to the dot, try sliding the colored paper (with the dot on it) side to side without moving your eyes. *Does the appearance of the dot change as you move the paper? Does it get easier to see?*

SCIENCE FAIR IDEA

Repeat this activity using different colored paper as the background. *Does changing the background color change the appearance of the dot? Does it change how high you can raise the wax paper before the dot becomes hard to see?*

OBSERVATIONS AND RESULTS

There were two important things to notice in this activity. The first point you may have observed was that when you focused on the spot next to the colored dot, the dot seemed to disappear. When you moved your eyes or head, however, the dot became visible again. The dot seemed to disappear because of how your eyes gather information about your environment. In this activity, the edges of the dot were blurred by the wax paper. This made it difficult for your eyes to use saccades to tell the difference between a point on the dot and a point right next to it. Because you were staring at the same place, your eyes weren't receiving any new information and the dot gradually faded into the background.

The second thing to notice in this activity was that you may have been able to raise the wax paper higher off the tabletop for some colors and still see the colored dot. This is because some of the colors (such as orange and red) are closer to each other in the color spectrum. This makes them more difficult to distinguish when the edges of the dot are blurred. Colors such as orange and blue are farther away from each other in the spectrum, and therefore, when you put a blue dot on the orange paper, you could probably see it more clearly as you raised the wax paper.

CLEANUP

Put away your materials. Throw out or recycle any unused scraps.

Can You See a Hole in Your Hand?

THINK YOU CAN ALWAYS BELIEVE YOUR EYES? TRY THIS SURPRISING ACTIVITY AND SEE HOW THE BRAIN CAN BE FOOLED WHEN YOUR EYES SEE TWO DIFFERENT THINGS!

Have you ever stopped to wonder why you have two eyes—but only see one image? Usually it is because your brain takes the information from each of your eyes and combines them, without you even noticing! However, sometimes your brain is too smart for its own good; it makes assumptions (or guesses) about the things you see. When your brain makes guesses, it sometimes makes mistakes, as it will do in this activity!

PROJECT TIME

10 to 20 minutes

KEY CONCEPTS

Perception
Vision
Optical Illusions

BACKGROUND

Why do you need two eyes to make one image? It turns out that you actually don't need two eyes for that—you can close one eye and still see pretty well. However, having binocular vision (two eyes working together) has some advantages. For instance, binocular vision gives you much better depth perception, increases the size of your visual field, and improves the accuracy of your vision.

When you want to look at something in front of you, you focus your eyes so that they are both pointing toward that object. (If the object is very close to your face, you may even go a little cross-eyed!) The cells at the back of your eyes—in their retinas—send signals to your brain about how much light and color they see. Your brain processes these signals to determine information such as the object's shape, distance from your face, and location in your visual field as well as the amount and direction of light in the field. By establishing these parameters for the object you are looking at, your brain is able to combine the information coming from your left and right eyes into one cohesive image.

Your brain is good (and fast) at what it does because it is designed to make intuitive assumptions. For example, your brain assumes that your eyes are focused on the same thing in your visual field. This is a very smart guess for your brain to make, because it is almost always true.

For this activity, you are going to trick your brain by having your eyes send different information about what you are seeing. When your brain tries to combine the images it receives from your left and right eyes, it will come up with some pretty interesting results!

MATERIALS

- A piece of white paper (8.5 by 11 inches, or 21.5 by 28 cm)
- Clear tape

PREPARATION

- Roll the paper along the longer side into a tube; the tube should be about the diameter of a quarter.
- Use a piece of tape to hold the paper in place.

PROCEDURE

- To start, choose a background to look at (a wall, a door, etc.) that is not white. Also, be sure you are in a well-lit space. This activity works best with a nonwhite background in a bright area.

- With both eyes open, raise your right hand so that your palm is facing toward your face, about 1 foot (30 cm) away from you.

- Look at your hand with both eyes open. Then use your left hand to alternately cover your left and right eyes while you continue to look at your right hand through the uncovered eye. Do this slowly at first. *As you slowly switch eyes, what do you notice first each time you switch which eye is uncovered? Do you notice what is behind your hand? Do you notice the lines on your hand?* (Just for fun: If you switch eyes fast enough, it may look like your right hand is moving back and forth a tiny bit!)

- Open both your eyes and keep them open. Lower your right hand and, using your left hand, place the paper tube up to your left eye (being careful with any sharp paper edges) so that you are looking through it as you would a telescope. *What do you see? Do you notice the paper tube first or the hole at the end of it? What do you notice about what your left eye sees compared with what your right eye sees?*

- Raise your right hand so that your palm faces toward you, then place it against the tube so that the outside of your pinky finger is touching the tube, about halfway down its length. Look straight ahead with both eyes open. *What do you see? Do you notice anything about your right hand? Can you change what you see by moving your right hand closer to or farther away from your face? What about if you move your right hand closer or farther away from the tube?*

- Keeping the tube and your right hand in place, try closing your right eye, then your left eye. (You may need a helper for this step if it is difficult to wink both eyes on your own.) *What is different about what your left and right eyes are seeing? What is the same?*

- If you saw something strange, try this: Without moving your right hand, slowly move the tube away from your face. See if you can continue to see the illusion, even as the tube gets farther away. *How far away does the tube have to be before you stop seeing the illusion?*
- Test what happens if you repeat this activity, but this time, look through the tube with your right eye. *Does this work for you with one eye but not the other, or does it work for both eyes?*

SCIENCE FAIR IDEA

Ask your parents and friends to try this activity and see if the illusion works better if they use their left or right eye to look through the tube.

OBSERVATIONS AND RESULTS

When you looked through the tube, did you see a hole in the hand pressed up against the tube?

So why do you see the hole in your hand? Whenever your eyes are open, your brain is working to combine the information coming from your left and right eyes into one image. This usually works remarkably well, and you don't even notice because both your eyes are usually looking at the same thing. In this activity, however, you are changing that one little fact: Your left and right eyes are seeing two different things! Your left eye is seeing a small circle of the world at the end of a tube, whereas your right eye is seeing your right hand.

When your brain combines the information coming from the left eye and the right eye, it looks something like this: Small circle of the world (from left eye) + right hand (from right eye) = small circle of the world going through your right hand!

If you tried the activity with both eyes, did you notice that one eye worked better than the other? Some people have a "dominant eye," similar to how they have a dominant hand. If you have a dominant eye, information coming from the dominant eye will take precedence over data from the nondominant eye. In this case, the tube illusion will work better when the person is looking through the tube using their dominant eye.

CLEANUP

Put the tape back where you found it.

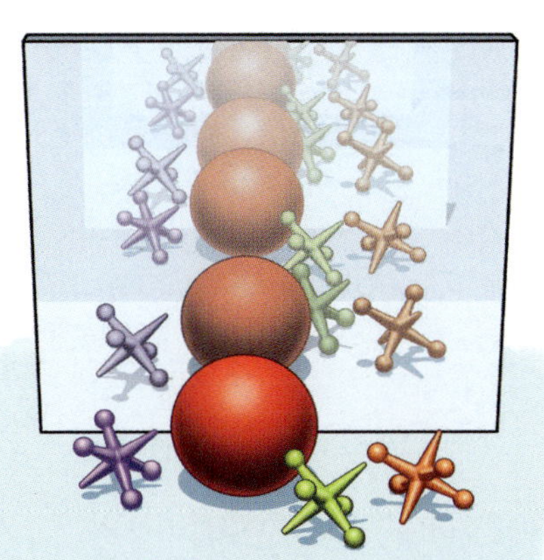

Can You Create an Infinite Number of Reflections?

HOW MANY REFLECTIONS CAN YOU MAKE? WITH JUST A COUPLE OF MIRRORS—AND THE CORRECT ANGLES—YOU CAN SEE (ALMOST) FOREVER. LEARN HOW THIS OPTICAL TRICK WORKS, AND TRY IT OUT AT HOME!

Can you imagine a bouncy ball that could bounce back and forth between two walls infinitely—that is, forever? Wouldn't that be amazing? What if, instead of a ball, light was bouncing between two walls, which were both covered in mirrors? Do you think that could bounce back and forth forever? Imagine if each light bounce added one reflection of an object in the mirror—for example, you! Would it look like there were an infinite number of "yous"? Perhaps you have noticed something like this in a fun house or a room with multiple mirrors. However, can we create an infinite number of reflections? Try this activity, and be amazed by the many images mirrors can create! Before you know it, you might be inspired to create some real works of beauty.

PROJECT TIME

15 to 20 minutes

KEY CONCEPTS

Reflection
Mirrors
Light
Infinity

BACKGROUND

The reason why you see objects is that light hitting these objects reflects back into your eyes (and then is perceived and represented as those objects by your brain). However, what happens if light coming from an object hits a flat mirror and is reflected (or bounced back) before it hits your eyes? Your brain, being unaware that the light was reflected, will reconstruct an image with the information it received, assuming the light traveled on a straight path from the object to the eye. The result is what you see in the mirror: an object that looks similar, but appears to be placed behind the mirror. We call this a *reflection* of the object. It is an *optical illusion*, a virtual image of a real object.

Mirrors, being shiny, reflect almost all the light hitting their surface. In addition, they have a very smooth surface, causing light to reflect in an orderly way. This allows your brain to reconstruct a clear image. High-quality mirrors reflect light especially well, but even high-quality mirrors absorb and scatter a small fraction of the light hitting them. As a result, a reflection is always a little dimmer and slightly less crisp than the image made with the same light reaching the eye directly.

Now, what image would your brain create if light reflected *several* times before hitting your eyes? Find out in this activity, and discover ways to create beautiful images!

MATERIALS

- Large wall mirror
- Small mirror with thin or no border
- Beads or other small, colorful objects (optional)

PREPARATION

- Collect your small mirror along with any colorful objects you might wish to use.

PROCEDURE

- Stand in front of a large wall mirror, looking into it. Make sure there are about 8 inches (20 cm) between you and the mirror.

- Hold a small mirror just under your eyes so that the reflective surfaces of the mirrors are facing each other.
- Place your index finger between the two mirrors, with your fingernail facing the large wall mirror. *Do you see the reflection of your finger in the wall mirror? Do you see the nail, the skin side of your fingertip, or both?*
- While looking at your index finger in the large wall mirror, briefly remove the small mirror and then put it back again. *Is what you see in the wall mirror different when you hold the small mirror in place? How is it different? Can you explain what you see?*
- Tilt the small mirror a little and watch what happens to the reflection(s). *Is there a particular position in which you can see very few reflections? What is the fewest number of reflections you see? Is there a position in which you can see a lot of reflections? How many can you see? Do they seem to go on forever?*
- Hold your small mirror in a position that allows you to see a lot of reflections. *Do you get the impression that the reflections are farther and farther away? How are the reflections that appear to be far away different from the reflections that appear to be close? Do they get dimmer or less sharp?*
- Take a step back from the wall mirror. *How does your image change if there is more space between the two mirrors?* Now get very close to the wall mirror. *Which distance results in more reflections?*

SCIENCE FAIR IDEA

Use the reflection properties you just explored and some other colorful objects, such as beads or other trinkets, to make a work of beauty. Then try to draw your creation and note the symmetry.

SCIENCE FAIR IDEA

Hold your small mirror vertically against the large mirror, at a 90-degree angle. It might help to rest the small mirror on a flat surface placed next to the wall mirror. Place your fingertip or a small, colorful object somewhere in the 90-degree angle between the two reflective surfaces. Level your eyes with the small mirror and look toward the vertical line where the two mirrors touch, so that you see the wall mirror and small mirror at the same time. *How many reflections do you see this time?* Reduce the angle between the two reflective surfaces to close to 60 degrees. *How many reflections do you see this time?* Repeat with angles of 45 degrees and 30 degrees. *Do you see a pattern? Can you explain what you observe?*

SCIENCE FAIR IDEA

If you have a kaleidoscope, look through it. *Can you explain how it works? How many mirrors do you think your kaleidoscope contains? At what angle do you think the mirrors are placed?* If you are allowed, you could try taking the kaleidoscope apart (knowing that you might not be able to return it to its original condition). (You can also use a kaleidoscope-making kit.) If you can take it apart, do so and explore the inside of the kaleidoscope. Then put it back together, changing one item at a time, and watch the result. *How does the resulting image change if you cover one mirror with black construction paper? How does it look when you cover more mirrors? What happens when you leave the eyepiece (the piece that you look through) off?* Try removing the piece containing the little trinkets and cover the tube with a colorful drawing. *Do you see anything? When you lift the tube a little, does an image appear? Why do you think this happens?*

OBSERVATIONS AND RESULTS

Did you get the impression of an infinite series of fingers?

When you looked at your finger in the wall mirror, you saw a reflection created by light bouncing off your finger hitting the mirror surface and reflecting back in your eyes. The finger appeared to be behind the mirror. Did you notice that you saw the nail side of your finger facing the mirror?

When you added the small mirror, you allowed light that was reflected on the wall mirror to hit the small mirror. This created a reflection of a reflection. You could not see this reflection of a reflection, as it was created behind the small mirror while you were looking in the wall mirror. However, you could observe a reflection of it as light from the reflection of a reflection hit the wall mirror and bounced back. A small fraction of this bounced-back light reached your eye, allowing you to see the reflection of a reflection of a reflection. Each bounce of light, back and forth, will add another reflection of a reflection to the count. The reflections in your activity probably looked as if they went on and on an infinite number of times (although given what we know about mirrors scattering and absorbing some of the light each time, we know that the number we could see is actually finite).

Did you notice that the small mirror also reflected the skin side of your fingertip, so you could see the skin side of your fingertip as a reflection of a reflection in the wall mirror?

Did your reflections get dimmer and less sharp as they appeared to be farther away? With each reflection, the mirror absorbs and scatters a tiny fraction of the light. After several reflections, the image fades out and you are no longer able to distinguish reflections. Increasing the distance between the mirrors will accelerate this fading, and thus result in fewer visible reflections.

You might have been able to block reflected light with your finger, preventing any further reflections to occur. In this case, you only saw one reflection showing your fingernail.

If you tried the science fair activity, holding one mirror against another at a 90-degree angle or at a smaller angle, you should have seen a circle of images appear. When the angle is an even division of 360 degrees (a full circle), you will get a beautiful pattern of reflections. Kaleidoscopes use both—the seemingly infinite reflections and the angled mirrors—to create beautiful images.

CLEANUP

Put away your materials. If you got the mirrors dirty, clean them off.

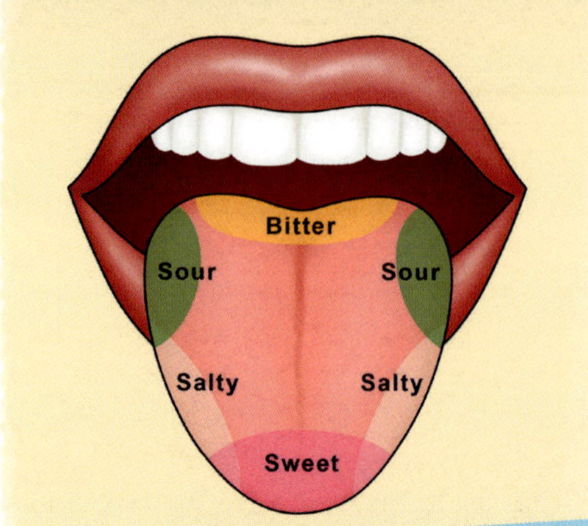

Sensory Science
Testing Taste Thresholds

EXPLORE THE LIMITS OF YOUR TASTE BUDS IN THIS SENSORY EXPERIMENT!

During the holidays, we often find ourselves surrounded by a wide variety of taste sensations. Have you ever wondered how well we sense different tastes? People are generally able to discern five basic tastes: sweet, umami (also known as savory), salty, sour, and bitter. Is it easier to detect some of these flavors compared with others? In this science activity, you (and maybe some friends or family) will find out by exploring your taste thresholds for sweetness, saltiness, and sourness. Get ready to find out how low you can go!

PROJECT TIME

50 to 60 minutes

KEY CONCEPTS

Taste
Perception
Senses
Food
The brain

BACKGROUND

Our sensory system for taste is remarkably sensitive. Not only can we detect substances at extremely low concentrations, we can also differentiate between molecular compounds that are closely related. For example, we can distinguish between different stereoisomers, which are molecules that are made of exactly the same components, but are mirror images of one another in their structure. The artificial sweetener aspartame is an example of this—it tastes sweet to us, but its stereoisomer (its opposite) does not.

This amazing sensitivity is made possible by our taste buds. Taste buds, located on small bumps on the tongue called fungiform papillae, are each made up of about 50 to 150 taste receptor cells. On the surface of these cells are receptors that bind to small molecules related to flavor. Through sensory nerves, the receptors relay the taste sensation information to the brain. This process allows us to discern five basic tastes.

MATERIALS

- Measuring spoons
- Water, preferably distilled
- 12 paper or plastic cups
- Permanent marker
- Kitchen scale or measuring spoons
- Granulated sugar or sucrose
- Table salt
- Vinegar
- Spoons
- Cotton swabs
- Paper towels
- Piece of paper and pen or pencil (optional)
- Taste-test volunteers (optional)

PREPARATION

- Pour 6 tablespoons (tbsp.) of distilled water into a paper or plastic cup. Add about 2.5 teaspoons (tsp.)—0.4 ounce, or 10 grams—of sugar and stir until the sugar is dissolved. This gives you a 10 percent sugar solution, approximately. Label the cup.
- Pour 2 tsp. of the 10 percent sugar solution into a new cup. Add 6 tbsp. of water to it and stir. This gives you a 1 percent sugar solution. Label the cup.

- Repeat this dilution process (diluting 2 tsp. of the previous solution in a new cup with 6 tbsp. of water) to make 0.1 percent and 0.01 percent sugar solutions. These are called serial dilutions. Be sure to label the two new cups. *What do you think is the lowest concentration you'll be able to taste the sugar in?*
- Repeat these steps (using clean utensils) to create salt solutions that have concentrations of 10 percent, 1 percent, 0.1 percent, and 0.01 percent. Label the cups. For 10 grams of salt, you can use 1.75 tsp. of salt. *What do you think is the lowest concentration you'll taste the salt in?*
- Again repeat the steps (using clean utensils) to create vinegar solutions that have concentrations of 10 percent, 1 percent, 0.1 percent, and 0.01 percent. Label the cups. Use 2 tsp. of vinegar initially. *What is the lowest concentration you think you'll taste the sour vinegar in?*

PROCEDURE

- Rinse your mouth with plain water and wipe your tongue dry with a clean paper towel. Dip a clean cotton swab into the 10 percent sugar solution and smear it all around the surface of your tongue. *Can you taste the sweetness?*
- Repeat the previous step to test the 1 percent, 0.1 percent, and 0.01 percent sugar solutions, rinsing your mouth and wiping your tongue before testing each solution. *Which solution is the lowest concentration at which you can still taste the sweetness?* This is your approximate taste threshold for sugar. You can write this down to remember later.
- Rinse your mouth with plain water and wipe your tongue dry with a clean paper towel. Dip a clean cotton swab into the 10 percent salt solution and smear it all around your tongue. *Can you taste the saltiness?*

- Repeat the previous step to test the 1 percent, 0.1 percent, and 0.01 percent salt solutions. *Which solution is the lowest concentration at which you can still taste the saltiness?* This is your approximate taste threshold for salt. You can write this down.

- Rinse your mouth with plain water and wipe your tongue dry with a clean paper towel. Dip a clean cotton swab into the 10 percent vinegar solution and smear it all around your tongue. *Can you taste the sourness?* Repeat this process to test the 1 percent, 0.1 percent, and 0.01 percent vinegar solutions. *Which solution is the lowest concentration at which you can still taste the sourness?* This is your approximate taste threshold for vinegar. You can write this down.

- *Were your taste thresholds (the lowest concentration at which you could still taste the flavor) the same for all three tastes, or did you have lower thresholds for some of them? Did the solutions that were tenfold more concentrated taste 10 times stronger?*

SCIENCE FAIR IDEA

Try repeating this activity using several volunteers. Compare your results. *Do some people generally have lower thresholds than other people? Is there a variation in which taste has the lowest threshold for individuals in the group?*

SCIENCE FAIR IDEA

Recruit several volunteers in different age groups to take this threshold-of-taste test. *Does taste threshold change predictably with age?*

SCIENCE FAIR IDEA

In this activity, you used tenfold serial dilutions to roughly establish your threshold of taste. Design a test to determine your threshold with higher precision. *What exactly is your taste threshold for sugar, salt, and vinegar?*

OBSERVATIONS AND RESULTS

Could you taste all of the 10 percent solutions, but none of the 0.01 percent solutions? Did the sugar solutions have the highest threshold, meaning you could only taste it in the more concentrated solutions, compared with the salt and vinegar solutions, which had lower thresholds?

For the sugar, salt, and vinegar solutions, the 10 percent solutions should be detectable by nearly everyone who tries the test, whereas almost nobody should be able to detect the 0.01 percent solutions because the concentrations are too low. The basic tastes of sweet, salty, and sour have different thresholds, or concentration levels, at which they can be detected. In other words, it is easier to detect some flavors at low concentrations compared with other flavors. Taste thresholds can vary from person to person. You may have seen that the sugar solutions were harder to taste at lower concentrations compared with the salt and vinegar solutions. In other words, the sugar solutions may have had a relatively high taste threshold compared with the salt and vinegar solutions. You may have also seen that the vinegar solutions had a lower threshold compared with the salt solutions (meaning the vinegar was easier to taste at lower concentrations), but this difference can be minor and may require testing by many individuals to see a clear trend.

CLEANUP

Put away your materials and wipe up any water that may have spilled. Dump your solutions down the drain.

THE SCIENTIFIC METHOD

The scientific method helps scientists—and students—gather facts to prove whether an idea is true. Using this method, scientists come up with ideas and then test those ideas by observing facts and drawing conclusions. You can use the scientific method to develop and test your own ideas!

Question: What do you want to learn? What problem needs to be solved? Be as specific as possible.
Research: Learn more about your topic and refine your question.
Hypothesis: Form an educated guess about what you think will answer your question. This allows you to make a prediction you can test.
Experiment: Create a test to learn if your hypothesis is correct. Limit the number of variables, or elements of the experiment that could change.
Analysis: Record your observations about the progress and results of your experiment. Then analyze your data to understand what it means.
Conclusion: Review all your data. Did the results of the experiment match the prediction? If so, your hypothesis was correct. If not, your hypothesis may need to be changed.

GLOSSARY

analysis: An examination of something to find out how it is made or works, or what it is.

anatomy: A science that has to do with the structure of living things.

artificial: Made by humans.

biology: A science that deals with living things and their relationships, distribution, and behavior.

diameter: A straight line that runs from one side of a figure and passes through the center.

dimension: One of three or four points determining a position in space or space and time.

illusion: Something that is false or unreal but seems to be true or real.

interference: Something that gets in the way as an obstacle.

perception: Understanding or awareness gained through the use of the senses.

physiology: A branch of biology that deals with the processes and activities that keep living things alive.

prerequisite: Something that is required before something else can be done.

puncture: An act of piercing with something pointed. Also, a hole or wound made by the act of puncturing.

receptor: A cell that receives a stimulus (such as light or heat) and activates an associated nerve to send a message to the brain and that may be grouped into a sense organ (such as a taste bud).

sensor: A device that responds to a physical stimulus.

threshold: The point at which a physiological or psychological effect starts to be produced.

ADDITIONAL RESOURCES

Books

McGregor, Harriet. *Slimy Science Experiments.* Minneapolis, MN: Bearport Publishing, 2021.

Sarcone, Gianni A, and Marie J. Waeber. *Shape Shifters.* Lake Forest, CA; Quarto Library, 2019.

Yi, Andrea Scalzo. *100 Easy STEAM Activities: Awesome Hands-On Projects for Aspiring Artists and Engineers.* Salem, MA: Page Street Kids, 2019.

Websites

Discovery Education
sciencefaircentral.com

Exploratorium
www.exploratorium.edu/search/science%20fair%20projects

Science Buddies
www.sciencebuddies.org/science-fair-projects/project-ideas/list

Science Fun
www.sciencefun.org/?s=science+fair

Videos

"Ask a Scientist: What Is an Optical Illusion?"
ny.pbslearningmedia.org/resource/nei-video-optical-illusion/ask-a-scientist-what-is-an-optical-illusion/, PBS Learning Media, 1:26.

"Optical Illusions"
ny.pbslearningmedia.org/resource/a268d5ec-a84d-49da-a125-590577318258/optical-illusions-diy-science-time/, PBS Learning Media, 26:39.

INDEX